PRAISE FOR !

Not for the faint-hearted, Trish Beɪ
Her poems burst from the pa&,
assaulting us with wit, a refreshing realism and a wicked imagination. This voice, this tone, with its deceptively easy humour and low-key social commentary, runs all the way through the poems as she recalls family occasions and key moments – often with unlaboured and deeply felt love, in some cases with abject sorrow, in others with outright hilarity or outrage. In addition, her evocations of place, home and nature are beautifully captured with much originality. A long time coming, this first collection is worth the wait. It has given the poet time to hone the tools of her trade, to fully develop her use of irony, her comedic timing, her intelligent framing of the political, religious and cultural mores she has encountered. This is a collection that will not disappoint on every reading!

– Ruth Carr

Trish Bennett beautifully captures the heart, soul and humour of the border counties. Even through the years of turmoil, her love for its natural beauty and people shine through that turmoil like a beacon.

– Marie Jones

Stench is an ebullient celebration of the human, the domestic and the natural world, an invitation to breathe in the myriad and diverse flavours of the poet's richly lived life, close to the border, a liminal space never far from her consciousness. Her poems combine an astute attention to structure and form, with an often hilarious and daring sense of inventiveness, are chockful of vivid images and turns of phrase, often magical in their originality and conception. Her language is precise, yet flowing, direct, yet ironic, emotional, yet unsentimental, and her deployment of regional border slang, idiom, myth and personal anecdote pay rich dividends. Her subjects range from childhood memory to the travails and joys of motherhood and marriage, from the beauty of the local landscape to the amorous exploits of bees and cockatiels. Trish Bennett's is a powerful and entertainingly optimistic voice, a humour-charged, irrepressible instrument that urges the reader to 'crank it up to MAX,' in the face of adversity. A wonderful, gloves-off, no-nonsense debut collection. It will do you the world of good to read it.

– Frank Farrelly

A meaty collection from a butcher's daughter who knows her border homeland well. Some poems make me cry. Others make me laugh loud, long, and hard. Parrots, dogs, cats, childer, bombs and bees all feature in their turn. A welcome space on my bookshelves for this beautiful collection.

– Réaltán Ní Leannáin

Trish Bennett's *Stench* announces a vibrant new voice in Irish poetry – one that is unafraid and bolshy; loud and clever. Bennett uses the vernacular of place to evoke the border country of her childhood and the lakelands where she now lives. The strength of that voice should not allow us to miss a vulnerability in these poems too, where the heart is lying bare on a flag stone, the bomb exploding on the page, and all of life is singing in the lines. This is a lyric taking poetry to a new place, taking on the romanticism of Yeats and saying 'Me Arse' much as Brendan Kennelly did. It is a loving account of a fierce woman who is living every day to its full, grabbing life by the horns and riding it!

– Maureen Boyle

In *Stench*, Trish Bennett gives us a potent admixture of bombs and bonhomie. She brings a warm forensic eye for cultural detail and is skilled at making charming things that are naturally sinister. Poignant and tender, these are poems of a troubled heart-place, delivered with a welcome, wicked eye-glint. Glorious stuff!

– Nuala O'Connor

Stench

in memory of my father, Joe Bennett,
who never let facts get in the way of a good story

and for my mother, Frances,
who's robbed lighting candles for us all

Trish Bennett

STENCH

ARLEN
HOUSE

Stench

is published in 2024 by
ARLEN HOUSE
42 Grange Abbey Road
Baldoyle
Dublin D13 A0F3
Ireland
Email: arlenhouse@gmail.com
www.arlenhouse.ie

ISBN 978–1–85132–330–2, paperback

International distribution
SYRACUSE UNIVERSITY PRESS
621 Skytop Road, Suite 110
Syracuse
New York 13244–5290
USA
Email: supress@syr.edu
www.syracuseuniversitypress.syr.edu

poems © Trish Bennett, 2024

The moral right of the author has been asserted

Typesetting by Arlen House

Cover image from www.dreamstime.com

Contents

Trouble Ahead
- 13   Border Child
- 14   The Technical School
- 16   Edge of the State
- 18   Reparation
- 19   Whellow
- 21   Monument to Home
- 22   UFO
- 23   Borderlines
- 25   Grafted
- 26   Kilty Relics
- 28   The Quiet Man
- 29   Moving On
- 30   Serving the Bishop in the House of the Parish Priest
- 31   Slices

Moonlight, Music, Love and Romance
- 35   Cupid's Arrow
- 36   Galway Crystal
- 38   Half Cut
- 40   The Gift
- 42   Recycling
- 43   The Slip
- 44   Frank
- 45   Port na bPúcaí
- 47   The Hag Stone
- 48   The Soul's Veneer
- 50   The Road Less Travelled at Annaghmakerrig
- 51   Tablet Under the Tongue
- 52   Taking Stock

54   Rituals
55   Sweet Spot
56   Morse Code

FACING THE MUSIC
59   The Day I Became a Royalist
62   Where the Wild Things Grow
64   Fuckery
66   Innisfree, Me Arse!
69   Raucous Wings
71   Valentine's 2020
74   My Post Lives the Life of My Dreams
75   Staying Safe
76   God Bless the Bees
77   Jailbreak
78   Corona Calypso
80   The Butcher's Daughter
82   The Stench of Poetry

84   *Acknowledgements*
87   *Notes*
88   *About the Author*

Stench

Trouble Ahead

Border Child

I come from bogs and butchers, reared
on a diet of rumour in a small kitchen, heated
by the polished copper pipe range.

I come from a childhood of fields, rivers and lanes
where my friends and I cycled our bikes
as we freewheeled towards freedom.

I come from cocoa before bed each night, reading
under cover of flashlight, being haunted
by stories of banshees and bogeymen.

I come from a place shaken by bombs, surrounded
by a river that sliced into them and us,
the bridges between, blocked by barricades.

I come from patrols, searches, red strobes
under cover of night, suspicion
of cars parked on lonely roads.

I come from adults being polite
to the flashlight in their faces, for fear
of bogeymen in the ditches.

The Technical School
inspired by Chalks *by Colm Keegan*

Flies to shite, we were,
my friends and I at six,
sneaking down the street
to be part of the gang,
our mothers' warnings ignored,
tell nawthin' – the rule.

I remember looking up
above that mountain of rubble
to the upstairs classroom.
Sunshine walls, a sky roof.

How much is a lie?
How much is truth?
They say memory twists
like the bars sticking out of the floor,
the jagged edge of a page torn.

The big ones flew up
the stairway of stones,
I drew the line at the climb.
In confession, we'd go to hell
but heaven was hunting for chalk.

We found white
where the blackboard had stood,
collected it all, and then we drew,
but had to dig to find a nugget
of green, yellow or blue.

Forty years on, that bomb
explodes across my torn page,
shards of the past
like those pieces of chalk
with slanted nubs,
the school was closed
mid-stroke.

Edge of the State

I was a child of the Troubles, but knowing no difference
was not a troubled child. I thought everyone's parents
were in the Civil Defence or Auxiliary Fire Brigade,
that every village had their roads to the north blasted,
schools bombed, windows shattered because they forgot
to open them to relieve pressure after the warnings came.
Mam crawled up the stairs to check on me in the cot,
convinced snipers in the northern hills behind our house
might have her in their sights. She put the snib on the door
after the night the British Army knocked on Nurse Flynn's
to say, *Lady, take in your key; you'd never know who's about
these streets.* Nurse Flynn, who'd Gardaí in digs asleep,
smiled and thanked the sergeant. The patrol realised
what side they were on when they reached the monument,
Seán Mac Diarmada, Republican leader, executed in 1916
so Ireland could have its freedom. Our village had roads
bombed, refilled, and blasted again until barricades came,
huge blocks of concrete clad with steel,
painted black and yellow with metal legs sticking out the top
like wasps with their wings snapped off.

My brother and I dreamed of *A-Team* night vision goggles
as we tried to spot army campfires on the Fermanagh hill
with binoculars. We thought it was normal to have patrols,
for cars to be stopped and searched, that it was routine
for Chinooks to drop soldiers in Allingham's field,
that every home had rubber bullet souvenirs.
When I was ten, I planned my escape from the bed
(in case strange men broke in), out the window
of my parents' room onto the galvanised roof at the back
of our shop, slide down the wall into Feely's yard
and out their gates like a bullet to get the guards.

The Gardaí bought steak in my father's shop.
With half his customers cut off and the bank on his back,
he bought a van and went on the road. When we hit
the teens, my brother and I were overjoyed to get
half-days from school as we took it in turn each week
to head on the forty-mile round-trip run via Ballyshannon
and Belleek to deliver meat to neighbours segregated
a few miles away in Kilcoo, Cashel and Garrison.
I waited impatiently while my father brought his forms
to Customs. On the northern side we were stopped
at gunpoint by the RUC, UDR and British Army.
He was asked again and again, *What's your name?*
Where are you from? Where are you going?
Dad slid open the door, watched them hoke
through his parcels of meat for incendiaries.
He worried they'd lift the few bottles of Powers
he'd hid for the Gorteen lads or the lock of cheap
Free State butter the women had told him to bring.

I grew to hate their red strobes circling *Stop*.
I wanted to know why he put up with it all.
I have no choice, he said. *Besides,*
they're men doing their jobs, men with families to feed
– just like him.

Reparation

We're on deliveries
at the last customer before home.
You're in no rush as you get the parcel of meat.
I won't be long, you say as you leave.

It's dark by six. The van windows start to steam.
I'm cold, bored. I use the torch you bought me
to light up my breath on the pane,
draw pictures, write my name,
suck butterscotch sweets,
shape their gold wrappers
into miniature versions of your cigarettes,
pretend to smoke.

After an age, you return.
Climbing into the van
you shout, *Thank you, Ma'am!*
to the silhouette who waves from the distant door.

I'm about to explode
when you set the tinfoil package
in the neutral zone of the middle seat
and start the engine to clear the smog.
You light up a fresh Silk Cut,
carefully write next week's order in the book
while I unwrap the offering.

The steam from that sweet, buttered boxty
lifts the mood between us.

WHELLOW

I sit at a desolate desk,
planted in an arse-paining plastic chair
beside cold bricks licked with gloss,
the Pantone of *I want to go home.*
Neither white nor yellow – whellow,
the colour of my face
as I turn to confront two pamphlets,
Questions and *Answers.*
A quick prayer pounds in my head,
Jesus, Mary and Joseph,
St Jude, patron of hopeless cases,
I know yiz were never ones for the books,
but please, please, get me through this.
I'll do Lough Derg,
barefoot, starving, with the beads.
I'll chant Hail Marys 'round the beds.

Coughs splutter from drowning friends
struggling to catch the saving line.
Teachers march to the notes
of swots shuffling papers.
They'd read Peig Sayers,
learnt their *cúpla focal.*
I learnt a few *focals* of my own
from my father
while we delivered meat
and supped *tae* in country homes.
Metal legs scrape the floor
as my chair rocks back and forth
to the beat of a distant clock that ticks
I – told – you – so,
I – told – you – so.

I open the answer book,
shuffle the pencil case,
put my best pen forward.
At least I know my name.

Monument to Home

We return home-home for the day
to pay our respects to another one gone.
On the way down from the funeral
we pass each other, stop, turn, stare,
recognise childhood friends by their eyes.

When we embrace, our voices echo off stone
like the way our feet used to clatter
off concrete pavements
on the race home in full flight from school.

We played hide-and-seek at the back of the houses,
tortured Gordon, Tommy-Andy and Pat,
for 10p mixes of cola bottles, fruit salads, black jacks,
liquorice laces, gobstoppers, false teeth.

Now, we've middle age mixes of arthritis, bad backs,
real false teeth. We stand in the street,
the Comanche plain and football field,
reminisce about the craic that Baltic winter,

going out after dark to sit on hay-stuffed 10–10–20 bags,
clinging tight to each other as our sled train rollercoaster
blasted down the snow-filled hill of the cratered road.

We talk, watch our children repeat the playtime climb
around the plinth of Seán Mac Diarmada.
No matter what troubles came, and they did,
Seán stood unmoved, his stone eyes fixed
on the hills of home.

UFO

My friend got an awful land
when he spotted Jacob Rees-Mogg
in the doorway of Johnston's drapers in Blacklion.
Seeing a man like that in Cavan
was like witnessing an alien landing.

Rees-Mogg, over to check the border,
had to be told where it was,
for you wouldn't realise unless you're local
with inbuilt border detection.

As children, we couldn't wait
for the first sliver of Christ on our tongue
so we could open the communion cards
from the aunts and uncles.

The cash inside used to bolster the fund
for our first Raleigh bike
from McNulty's in Enniskillen.
Once bought, we were driven to the border,
let out to cycle past the Customs,
told to ignore the *Stad*,
Sure, they'd never stop a child.

We grew up amongst checkpoints, guns
and cratered roads,
never had to think which side we were on
until Rees-Mogg lands into Blacklion
to ask where the border was
as if there were never any Troubles.

Borderlines

This land is sword-scarred from centuries of invasion.
Vikings, Chieftains, Kings and Queens,
come and go.

The scores they leave take time to heal.
People still fight over the language we speak
or the colour of the cloth on a pole.

We who live on the wound line
have been sliced apart
by those who wield the sword.

In the Troubles,
armed forces severed arteries
to our villages and towns.

For security, they said,
as parents watched their blood drain
in planes, trains and boats.

Now frackers come
to sit in suits
in air-conditioned rooms.

They circle contours on maps as they plan
to drain the innards from the Geopark,
the lifeblood of our land.

Frackers don't know what it is
to be reared amongst blue daub, bog
and limestone hills,

to cycle full-tilt down a grass-lined lane
or Sunday stroll through the woods
of Glenfarne Demense,

to eat wild strawberries from ditches
while the roast is in the oven
or take a boat on a soft-spoken day

to fish our glacial lakes;
Lough Melvin, Lough Erne and MacNean,
to breathe that brisk heather air

at the top of Cuilcigh or Thur,
to feel connected to God
in the terrible beauty of this place.

Frackers fence off test bores,
know the drill to spin.
For security, they say,

and promise
when all's fracked
they'll restore our borderlands.

We don't believe.
We've heard this line before.

Grafted

The Leitrim hills are choked by Sitka spruce,
trees planted when we were saplings,

all of us bred
to take root elsewhere.

As the years roll by, fresh folk graft in
from densely-packed places,

bring colourful accents to quiet streets
and warmth into damp halls.

They paint bright shades over faded patterns
as the new take up the old mantle.

When the spruce is cut and harvested,
the hills see light, can breathe

for the first time in thirty years.
The pale wounds of our land begin to heal,

but it won't be long
before the forestry machines return

to clear the unwanted
and plant again.

Kilty Relics

In the eighties, the far-out relations breezed in our door
to trace their roots and *ooh!* and *aah!* our home,
one hundred and fifty years old – a museum,
my brother and I on display; *Twentieth Century Irish Teens*.
Mam stuffed them with *tae*, tart and treacle bread,
Go-wan! Go-wan! A little bit more,
while Dad dished out hot ones and stories galore.
Later, he drove down dung-filled roads,
made them stop to let the fairies cross.
They hopped out with flashes, white innocent smiles
and pressed roses from hedges in their Ireland guides.

In the graveyard by Lough Melvin's shore,
Dad had no clue where the ancestors lay.
A minor point – they'd come all this way.
He showed them a grave by the limestone wall,
question after question came
until they asked, *Why the unmarked plot?*
His answer nailed the questions shut.
When people left long ago,
'twas tradition to send money home
for a decent wake and a good headstone.

They called to a cottage on the return.
A mound of stones in the field beside
was all that remained of their ancestors' lives.
My father spoke to the man at the door,
They've come from the States, we can't disappoint,
so the man became a far-out cousin,
threw himself into the role.

Come in! Come into my home!
Your great grandmother's bed's in the lower room
where she knelt every night to say her prayers.
She sat here, at the hearth,
Sit down! Sit down in her chair.

He gave them a piece of the hearthstone
– a relic to share.

The far-out relations breezed home with tears in their eyes,
and rose-tinted pages in their Ireland guides.

THE QUIET MAN
i.m. Young Pat McGriskin

After mass each Christmas Day, he filled the chair
in the corner of our kitchen, *tae* in hand, to watch
Mam and I peel strips off the spuds and each other.

He came armed with good cleaning cloths from London,
a slab of salmon, wine, chocolates and a bag of DVDs
packed with enough action to blast us into the New Year.

Mam would roar, *I never saw yiz a day better!*
over the rat-a-tat-tat of the opening scene, leaving
to the screams of some poor sod getting stabbed in the eye
with a carrot.

Pat returned for good, settled into the home he'd built
in the village, *céilí'd*, played cards, threw his hand
to any job. That winter, he slipped and broke his leg
in the bad frost,

my father picked his way along the icy path,
Florence of the ash plant on his daily mission
to deliver messages and homemade bread.

Pat recovered, and Dad began to slip. Pat persisted
with the visits, tried to get the rise, while others drifted,
unable to watch my father's slide from craic to quiet.

When Pat died, we never told, for Dad was leaving too.
Pat left long before his time, yet we see him still,
tae in hand, smiling from the corner

as my father spins yarns at the table.

Moving On

Canon and Bishop compete with a cackle of priests
to dictate high mass for their pious deceased.

The altar boy swings his thurible. Clouds of incense release
to spaced out family flooding front seats.

A scrum of nuns sits a few pews below,
rattling beads in a mahogany row.

A toddler runs wild when free from her leash.
Her mother's on her knees, praying for peace.

Cousins speckle throughout, shades of black into grey,
depending on what could be got for the day.

Tissues and tears when the sermon begins.
Priests remember the good, never the sins.

Boiled sweets do the rounds between musty old coats
as upstanding men have the craic telling jokes.

Laughs turn to coughs to sober the mood
because there at the front, boxed in between pews,

lies their friend, a man who once laughed too,
in stitches now as he awaits the final move.

Serving the Bishop in the House of the Parish Priest

At eighteen
it was an honour.
Even better
to get a second run
out of my expensive Debs dress,
handmade from royal blue
satin-look polyester,
the layered skirt lengthened
to below-the-knee,
respectable.

I channelled Alexis Carrington
with those *Dynasty* shoulders
as I was fussed in and out of the room
to serve plates piled with food
prepared in the back kitchen
by the village women.

Black-clad men gathered around the feast
as if it was the last supper,
every priest was revered
like a saint,
the bishop,
God himself.

SLICES
i.m. Joe Bennett, master butcher

You caught me today at the turn
of that tight hill before home.

When the sun dissected the trees,
a slice of the past shone,

that summer's day in our shop
your suet-soft hands held the knife

as you dissected a liver
to show me fluke.

Keep a tight grip, you said,
so it won't slip as you slice.

You carved the disease out,
diced the rest for cats.

I could've been a surgeon in another life,
you remarked, and we laughed.

The memory fades,
replaced by the last sigh from your lungs

as the grip tightens
around my heart.

Moonlight
Music
Love
and
Romance

Cupid's Arrow

MTV blared in that room
thick with smoke from wacky-baccy.
I'd my eye on Biker Boy for a while,
ponytail, Levis, black boots,

sitting perched on the arm of a couch
on the other side of the room.
Other girls had him in their sights,
I needed something to catch his attention.

A six-inch honed hacksaw blade
with a handle of tightly-wound tape
lay between bottles and bongs
on the no man's land of the table.

In my full-to-the-gills state
I recalled throwing star training
a Belfast ninja ex-boyfriend had taught me,
lifted the knife by its tip, let it rip ...

It lodged deep into the dry-lined wall
to the right of Biker Boy's ear.
When he looked across and said, *Wow!*
I knew I'd nailed my target.

Galway Crystal

You held me with champagne
in a Galway crystal glass.
The light fizzed through its facets
and danced a sparkling ring.
No dawter a mine'll be on time,
make him wait, you said.
Your brother, our driver, obeyed.

We parked at the church
set into the mouth of a bad turn.
The Blessed Virgin,
mounted on granite,
stood guard outside.
Celtic crosses scattered
on the grave hill behind.

To the side, a stream flowed
under the stone-bridged road,
feeding the lake in front,
from where two swans watched
as you opened the door
and held my hand
to support my high-heeled step.

You carried the weight of my frock,
the countryman's Gok Wan.
I held tight to my autumn bouquet
as we strolled into that place
built on unyielding rock,
a slope to its aisle.

The Coolin began.
My bridesmaid led the march,
you slipped your arm in mine,
laughed as you led me on.
Flower girls ran in a fizz to grab hold
and tow us up that hill
to the green-marbled altar.

You smiled
as you sacrificed me there,
to face the music – half-cut.

Half Cut

We watched the 'How to' DVD.
Any eejit can do that, says I,
and me still drunk from the night before.
It started well.
Halfway through, the hangover set.
When the shakes began
and I fought the urge to get sick,
the clippers took off,
mowed a patch of hair
a breath from his ear.

Himself locked the clippers away,
my career cut short
on account of that baldie he got
so many years ago.
These days, he lets his hair grow
till his eyes disappear under a grey hedge.
I think of my father, how he used to say,
There'll be no barbers at that buck's funeral.

Himself has important folk to meet,
and him with a head like a mountain sheep.
Will you do me? he says.
Well ... It's an offer I can't refuse.
I lay newspapers down,
sit him on the stool.
The light's too low,
so I put the head torch on,
hands-free to swing a plastic cape,
the thick black of a body bag
around his neck.

He reads the 'How to'
as if it will enlighten me.
Start at the back
and work your way round
to the front and sides.
I stand by his side to brush his hair.
He doesn't see my hands,
hands that haven't held a vodka in years,
shaking again. This time, with fear.
I take a deep breath,
grab hold of his ear
with the grip a farmer gives
to the horn of a ram,
set the clippers to number two
and hit the switch to shear.

Are there arteries in the head? I ask
as the clippers take off on the mow,
a bottled demon released.

The Gift

The day I lost you, I lay cursed, covered in blood,
curled up in a heap on flagstone tiles.
You left a gift to help me heal.

I use it today.
Rough sparks ignite as the self retreats,
releases the muse
to chisel into that place
where hearts break,
face pain, again and again.

I would give back every vowel and verb,
adjective and metaphor,
for time and place, love and loss.
I'd give back the awards, the grants,
the chances.

I'd lose every word to keep you in this world,
to smile in relief at the sound of your first cry,
to smell that baby smell of you
and wipe those wet blonde curls
you'd have from your father's side.

I'd hold you skin-to-skin
as you opened your eyes
for the first time.

I'd give back this gift,
every damned letter of it,
to see you grow up
to be a gangly youth
chasing your father through fields
on scrambler bikes.

I'd stand to watch
without the words to express
how my heart swells with pride.

Words are all I have.
I tap at the keys to ignite that spark you left,
chisel into that place, that day, that pain
on the grey flag of my heart.

RECYCLING
for Sarah

In the noughties
the Russians recycled an old spacesuit,
launched Mr Smith, the suit-satellite.

SuitSat Smith circled the earth for a year or two,
his signal grew weaker and weaker
until his battery died.

On the day they declared him dead
you entered my world
to orbit my life, morning, noon and night,

your battery was charged by boobs and naps.
In the early days,
before your words came,

you cried to be lifted,
gyrated into my hip
to signal what you wanted.

The seasons turn and you grow strong.
My charge doesn't hold
as it used to

as my signal slowly fades.
I'm not afraid, for I know
on the day my suit dies

another new cycle begins.

The Slip

Seconds underwater,
you, an auburn mermaid,
hair adrift in graceful panic,
I freeze in horror.
Can you surface on your own?
No.
You are sinking further.
Piddle water, twelve inches deep,
six feet between us,
might as well be sixty.
I race to you on slippy knees
cursing that toddler pool
as I fish you out,
my catch of the day
in pink and white polka dot.
First aid I'd thought forgotten kicks in,
expel the water with a slap to the back.
You spit a cry when your little lungs fill with life,
limpet-grip me as my arms blanket you.
It's ok, baby, Mammy's here.
Tears stream down my cheeks.
I breathe deep,
try to keep calm
in case I give you
the fear.

FRANK

So, you've just the one, you say.
I don't flinch now like I used to
when your words would slice
and I would make an excuse to get away,
to hate you with your easy three.

A flare lit up my womb for enough time
to set us alight over names and what he'd look like.
Would he have his father's curls or my side's teeth
when there'd have to be a lock pulled.

When the flare fizzled out I became so filled with loss
that my ovary, the one that swung to the left,
tried to fill the void by rearing a Frankenstein cyst
on itself.

The size of an orange with teeth and hair,
the surgeon said,
after he'd cut Frank
and the rebel leftie out.

So, you've just the one, you say.
I don't flinch now like I used to
when your words would slice
and I would make an excuse to get away.
I just say, *Yes,* like I had a choice.

PORT NA BPÚCAÍ
The Ghost Jig

As the darkness descends before Macnas,
don't stand too close to the Tiger-Mammy
blown-in on the Celtic breeze,
for she has brought her children to see the parade.
She has entitlements. They've been there since three.

Don't say that your husband's people
have been there for three hundred years
or that you've travelled for half a day
so your daughter can see the parade,
for the Tiger-Mammy's Galwegian now.
This gives her the right to insult you *as Gaeilge*.

You've learnt school Irish too, enough
to sell foals at Maam Cross in your youth
and to understand all she says, but you just smile
and wave. You smile and wave because you know
that the Mammy's about to blow.

Her young, high on Haribo Worms,
race out over the road. She roars
and they leap into their father's arms.
He wrestles one to his shoulder, the other, his hip,
dances a jig as he loses it.

Your daughter – high on her Daddy's shoulders,
gets a smiley-face sticker from a Macnas girl
in a rainbow hat. The crowd surge in a wave
as the darkness lifts with the eerie light from a ghost ship.
A puppet dog at the bow opens his mouth,
reminds you of Judge from *Wanderly Wagon*.

You chew Aunty Nellie's bonbons to the beat of the drums
watch a giant bearded druid at the stern of the boat
with pearlescent eyes that blink
as he waves his savage hands.
Black-skulled Púcaí in ashen white robes,
thread so slow they seem to float
through billowing smoke.

A lighthouse shines across a sea of heads,
dancers shout a rhythmic chant, swing monster gulls
like wands to cast a clearing spell.
When the banshee rises from the mist of her dress,
Tiger-Mammy and family have vanished,
blown out by the gale of Port na bPúcaí.

The Hag Stone

The dog starts to yelp before we open the door.
When released on the beach, she circles in laps so fast
her arse passes her front on the turn.
My daughter puts black glittered wellies on.
We head for the rocks beyond the sea wall, scan
shale for shells and stones for her bucket.

The wind whisks sand, stings our faces in waves.
It's like the Sahara, she says.
Can you look for a stone with a natural hole?
I've read that hag stones have power; they bring good luck.
If the hole's big enough you can glimpse the otherworld,
but it won't reveal itself until you're ready.

Her father's lost in his world as he picks his steps
along black rocks to stand and look out to Aran.
The Atlantic opens her mouth, foams into land
in rows of seven roars. There's something about
the way that brown-sod bog rolls down to meet
the scattered rocks of Spiddal beach

that reminds me of backpacker days in Australia,
standing in gobsmacked awe at the sight of the rainforest
meeting the reef at Cape Tribulation. A lifetime away
from this place, this rock, where I sit
to watch the dog trail my daughter and sniff
as she gathers cockle and mussel shells and pebbles.

I've wandered for years
not knowing what a hag stone was
or even what I was searching for.
When I gaze through the salt-spray breeze
on this sacred day
I know I've found it.

The Soul's Veneer
Dermot Healy Photographic Exhibition,
Fierce Moon Festival, Manorhamilton, Co. Leitrim, 2017

The mother and I went home that night
filled with the glow of the fierce moon,
there's less of a grip – slow down –
by the wood,
the leaves have started to fall, Mam said.
out of the trees, a fox leapt
onto my road
I thought it a dream
I know it is true;
herself gave out
that's not a ferret,
that's a mad-looking fox,
he's meant to be red
– not white like a ghost
last night on
a different road,
he jumped out again
wore a moon coat dappled with oak,
those feral eyes

your publisher spoke
about your life and work,
*it takes generations to domesticate the fox
but Dermot will always be safe,* he said.
I saw
– your life in a parade of snaps
in a place where I worked at another time,
when I wrote words of a different type. Now
the workshop is clean
as if polished white – reborn,
and me standing there in fear of rebirth,
you, framed at the spot,
where the sander stood, a machine
that transformed the rough wood
to paper-thin sheets of polished veneer –
I smelt wood shavings falling like leaves,
into a mound where your feet would be if you
leapt from sepia into my path,
daring me.

The Road Less Travelled at Annaghmakerrig

I take a new path into the woods,
realise I don't know this place,
feel watched from high
by lines of lofty pine and spruce.

There's no sound of traffic.
The signal has dropped,
there's no connection.
I fear what comes in the silence.

I catch a strong scent of fox in one spot,
wish I'd brought my father's plant for protection.
Hoverflies masquerade as bees in a bid to scare.
I recognise their two-winged fakery and leave them be.

When I sink deep into muck,
I'm glad I've dubbed the boots
for they've carried me dry out of sheughs
from the first time I wore them hungover

to see the remains of the Sunderland plane
in the Bluestacks of Donegal,
to these settled days when I stroll the lane
with daughter and dog.

I pray to the spirits of alder, ash and oak
to guide me home, for inspiration has stuck,
and it's past lunch. Bird shit streaks bark

at the tail end of the trees
as they clear to reveal,
I'm back on track,
not far from the Big House.

Tablet Under the Tongue

Never one for the busy road,
he preferred the country lane
where he told wild tales of his youth
and folk who once lived in ruins we'd pass.
He'd untangle my woes, often adding more
before we reached the head of Raheelin.
He stopped halfway up the hill
to put a tablet under the tongue
for the heart that never killed him,
but broke so many times
because of the brother and me,
though we never killed him either.

These days, the daughter walks with me,
the dog on the lead pulling.
I use the plant that her Granda made
with the copper pipe end.
It click-clacks the lane before we go off-road
to avoid being clipped by cars.
We pick our way through cow-tracked fields
as I tell wild tales of my youth,
try to untangle her woes, often add more
before we reach the shores of Lough Erne.
On the way home we rest at the rise,
share Polo mints like her Granda used to do.
I tell how he'd stop halfway up the hill
to put a tablet under the tongue
for the heart that never killed him,
but broke so many times
because of the brother and me,
though we never killed him either.

Taking Stock

Every time I strain the stock,
her words grate in my mind,

Keep the stock, ladies.
It's full of vitamins.
Use it again for soups and gravies.

I'd have loved that class
but for the way she tore on a bias
that left me in shreds.

She took my notebook
with the collie dog on every page,
moved me to her desk – the anti-pet.

We sat so close that our knees brushed.
I was a pincushion pierced by her tongue
until I told my parents I could take no more.

My father said, *Stand up for yourself.*
If that doesn't work we'll sort her out.
I lay awake the night before

I stood my ground to say,
I'm leaving.
Give me my notebook back.

Her tack changed to one of praise.
You're not going.
You're one of my best.

My parents know,
let me go
or they'll deal with you.

Get out of my sight! she shouted
and threw the book – too late
to unravel what she'd sewn.

I tucked it into the pocket
of my home-sewn skirt
as I left.

I'm a mother now with a girl of my own.
I've taken stock of that time,
used it again,

my child is nourished
– strong.

Rituals

I stand in the corridor of power
and face the congregation.
The sun illuminates the island altar.
Solid walls echo the sizzle of pans steaming hymns.
Often, my chant – not quite Gregorian,
catching the custard on the cusp of a curdle.
We'll leave soon, and I will miss this chapel of a kitchen,
the soul of a borrowed place we never called *home*.
Our brown boxes, taped to escape,
surround the naked dresser in scribbled rows.
Whisk in hand, I plant my feet firmly,
seize a tight grip on the bowl
as the final liturgy begins.

Sweet Spot
Lower Lough Erne viewed from Claragh Road, Blaney

Each morning
I grasp the curtains with tired hands
and fling my arms wide.

Rings rattle in retreat on their rail
as the Fermanagh Monet fills my frame.
I await the lift like a cradled child.

Sun tackles showers on in-between days,
sprinkles of rainbow are cast upon isles.
Boats speckle the lough like white chocolate chips

rippling the mirrored reflection of sky.
My eyes soak it up as the day kicks in,
I float away on a natural high.

Each night I take a closing fix.
Through the shadows,
Irvinestown twinkles a smile,

a handful of jewels
draped on the end of one arm
while I perch content on the other side.

Morse Code

I was born on wheels, never reached a full stop
till I found a bungalow of tile, dash and block
that blends into the bark of ash and beech,
arm-chaired on a hill near Lough Erne's shore.

The kitchen window frames fuchsia, roses, trees,
the lough, as it rests in the valley below,
where geese return each year to mate,
swim with ducks, and swans
who love themselves so much
they clap their own applause.

On the back of the rise beyond,
the hospital lies flat,
behind that, the statue of old Cole
like its chimney stack.

As good days turn to dusk
I stand at the sink
to watch the amber glow stretch itself out
until the flat cap of Cuilcagh is haloed,
before it settles into the sods of my people,
Fermanagh, Cavan, Leitrim.

On my return at night, our outside lights,
high on the far-off hill,
spot my wheels on the lower road,
dot Morse code between the trees
to call me home.

FACING THE MUSIC

The Day I Became a Royalist

The memory of that day is still sweet,
the way the sun filtered through hedges

beginning to explode
with blooms of hawthorn and chestnut,

the coconut trace
that floated up from yellow-bubbled whin,

the excited buzz from her fans
humming as I set to work.

Deaf as beetles they were,
yet they danced their tales

while their friends watched
and felt the vibrations.

I longed to dance too
but my rebel feet refused.

I looked the part,
in fact I was smoking

with all the right gear
to meet a queen.

No high fashion, fascinators,
stilettos or frocks,

demure in loose white,
a veil over my face and gloves.

The roar arose from the crowd,
herself was close.

Royal guards drew lances,
made charges as if to say,

Your kind's not welcome here.
I worked on, ignored the line

like my father before
when I was a child.

When Her Highness appeared
in my frame of view,

maybe it was the alien look of her dress
poured out in layers like dark chocolate

or perhaps it was her long legs
that made her look huge.

She walked that confident walk
of a girl at the top.

Her retinue fussed,
showed respect.

While her signature scent was strong,
they remained happy, loyal, content.

My senses captured it all
in a way no camera could,

that joy as I watched them dance and hum,
the Chinook noise from drones,

the scent of our land collected, condensed,
mind-stamped into my memory cells

that brought me home to my childhood days
when my brother and I

dug sections of gold
on our father's return.

The memory's still sweet
of that day when I turned

on meeting the Queen
of Apis mellifera mellifera,

my black honey bees.

Where the Wild Things Grow

When the neighbour owned our home,
the street was bleached, not a weed to be seen.
Since the bees arrived, we've set the garden free
to see how far she roams.

Wild vetch grows through geranium and rose.
Damsels, dragons and hoverflies arrive in droves.
Wasps eat greenflies on leaves,
while ladybirds have orgies on the verge.

The daughter says we've at least two hundred snails.
She's named them all as she blings their shells with varnish.
A common frog lives in the drain. There's nothing common
about the way we talk to him each day.

Pheasants pop into the field (a place once sprayed)
as it waves with flax, cuckoo and clover.
Will Feral, the cat, moved in,
helps himself to mice from the compost bins.

When the long winter's done
our bees work an untended plot
of dandelion pollen for their young
before the hawthorn kicks off in May.

They survive on nectar from under the leaves
of the overgrown laurel during the drought in June.
July arrives in all its bloom when brambles
and robin-run-the-hedge rule.

Bumblebees moon fuzzy bums
from the depths of rhododendrons.
The bees swarm but don't leave,
they're onto a good thing here.

We cheer when Clematis montana,
that wandering rogue,
rises to sit pretty-in-pink
at the top of the three-storey pine.

A rainbow of buddleias
goes mad with growth
when summer sun opens their butterfly shows
of painted ladies, peacocks and admirals.

Magpies and crows dispose of our scraps,
leave just enough for the robin.
The hedges are stuffed
with full-bellied finches and thrushes.

Hedge-cutting's banned in autumn
until the bees have refilled their stores.
Ivy musk wafts from the apiary
as workers return overloaded with pollen.

Nanny Hedgehog arrives,
stuffs her face for a week with cat kibble.
She rolls into a spiky ball to scare the dog
before leaving to hibernate.

Even though the neighbour despairs
of our untamed ways,
we know
it does the world of good.

Fuckery

Our first home housed a loved-up crowd,
ourselves, and two cockatiels, Honda and Hank,
who saw the lust we had for each other
and decided to breed.

Their enthusiasm led to the sitting room
resembling a scene from Hitchcock's *The Birds*.
On opening the door, ten chicks dive-bombed
from wall-mounted roosts.

We'd to turn up the volume on *Friends*
to drown their hiss-shagging on top of the telly.
We sold all to a breeder but kept Wee Bert,
her orange cheeks ablaze in permanent embarrassment.

There wasn't a bad bone in her body
except for the one in her gammy wing
from that time she got jammed
behind the radiator.

We returned from honeymoon to a house
overrun by mice. Poor Bert was poisoned
when she pecked mouse droppings.
I wanted to catch and release,

but Himself was out for revenge.
The mice weren't fooled by cheese in traps,
Cadbury's Mini Rolls their Achilles heel.
Forty-five dead. I've not bought a Mini Roll since.

Twenty years and three houses later,
summer switches on and our bees multiply
in swarms. We've neutered the cats,
for given half a chance they'd be at it too.

Flaming heat brings flying ants
to cloud the roof on balmy evenings.
They find gaps in the chimney, emerge at the cooker,
fuck-fest in the dining room.

We've read on Google that incense repels.
It's mid-July, thirty degrees outside,
humidity's up to ninety,
our range is set to two hundred and fifty degrees C,

the house smells like a knocking shop,
the pair of us are sprawled in a swelter of incense and heat
to watch *The Walking Dead* on TV
while flying fuckers blaze out from the chimney.

INNISFREE, ME ARSE!
with apologies to WB

Small cabins are not ideal; a king-size bed,
an island kitchen, they'll never fit in.
Clay and wattle are all well and good
but you're better with the block.

Insulate like the Swedes
for the autumn wind whips across that lake,
skins ash and beech to cover paths and choke the gutters,
brings with it Canadian Geese, who come
to keep you up all night
with their honk-bonk orgy by the shore.

Skeletal cats move in,
take over chairs and laps, purring and pats,
turn into big brutes that drag in prey
and lap milk night and day
with low sounds by the door.

Linnets won't get a look in
with the magpies and the crows
who sit in trees to *Gogglebox* your windows
like reality TV
as they wait to steal the food
you leave for tits.

For evenings filled with wings,
get an African Grey.
He'll dive-bomb dinner
with a *kaw* and a *kak*,
shout, *me, arse!*
throwing scraps to the dog – barking mad.

Don't plant the nine bean rows
for steroid-pumped slugs
the size of an ink-stained thumb
will scoff your hopeful shoots.
As for slug traps filled with stout,
those louts'll down the lot
then slime home on beer bellies
lost in the plot.

If you love *Game of Thrones*,
get that hive of honey bees.
The summer's filled with battles
and drones in death throes
after mating with the queen.
Poor lads, they come as they go.

A bee-loud glade's
not the place to live alone
for it's far from cricket song
when you dangle at an angle
on a ladder saying prayers
as you cut a branch of brown-winged leaves
that breaks to a roar
and a swarm of twenty thousand bees
drop slow
into a cardboard box
balanced on the head of your only help
– a passing ten-year-old.

Walkers stroll down your road
on their way to the shore,
stand to admire the birds and the bees
in your garden's flowering trees.

They don't notice the cats
giving death stares from below
till your little dog barks,
Rip their heads off!
and your parrot wolf-whistles
like a sailor out the door.

I hope they feel your peace
in their deep heart's core.

Raucous Wings

When you live in the sticks
you'd think there'd be peace.

Not a hope this week
with the racket of winged things.

House martins crowd telephone lines,
swoop down in a chitter-chatter.

A village of starlings
land in the cherry tree.

Their ruckus upsets the tits enough
to flit their feeder

and return to defend their perches.
The Catalina's returned

to do laps of the lough,
bringing back the sounds of the '40s.

She takes the turn so low
her engines throom-throom over our home.

She looks like she'll belly-slap Lunny's hill,
but no, she glides on to land at St Angelo.

When she vrooms over the room
on the umpteenth turn

I imagine our lane,
a rough track then,

fit only for horse and cart
and hardy folk.

The noise of herself
and her Sunderland friends

flying low to land
on their Atlantic return.

As they roar over
their stone-walled homes

the women grab the beads
and bless themselves

when their Sacred Hearts
are rattled.

Valentine's 2020

The daughter wanted to see the Champs-Élysées,
but instead of heading to Chanel and Dior,
we wandered into a shop beside the toilets
that sold bows and arrows, knives and air rifles.
Even the headless manikin doll
wore a fur coat and a bulletproof vest.
A buck, the cut of Ron Perlman
in a fur-trimmed goose-feather-jacket,
sat camouflaged into a black leather armchair.
Ron just stared when I said, *Bonjour.*
The whole shebang made the daughter nervous.

Himself was in his element, strode to the counter
to make his first attempt at Belfast-French,
bawn-joore.
The saleswoman replied in English, *You English?*
I speak no English.
Irlandais, Bell-faast, says Himself.
Aah, Belfast! I am from Beirut! she said,
as they used Google translate
to bond over troubled places.
Do you have throwing knives
– lawn-say the kudo?
Yes, we have them in stock, the best stainless steel
– not cheap, we're almost sold out to the tourists.

Beirut rapid-fire spoke to a man on a walkie-talkie,
removed the fur coat from the doll, put it on
and left us to Silent Ron, who chewed his cheroot
as he scoped us. When she returned,
the daughter leaned over to whisper,
Where's the coat? Is there a man out there
dressed like Cruella?

Beirut produced a brute of a blade
with all sorts of fancy gimmicks,
for only one hundred and fifty euros.
To my relief, Himself thought it too highfalutin,
so we headed to the only place he'd pinned
on my birthday tourist trail
– The Armoury at The Bastille.

This shop was hardcore stocked,
Glocks, Browning's and AK-47s.
Being a butcher's daughter
I was drawn to the assortment of steel.
I laughed at the time, but in retrospect,
wish I'd bought those books on *Living Off-Grid*
and *How to Survive the Apocalypse.*

Himself purchased his souvenirs, treated us to
pocket Swiss, tissue-wrapped by a lad,
the spit of an accountant.
The accountant said, *You'll have no issue
since these are for personal use.*
All the same, Himself packed them into my case,
trusting the border woman to deal with customs.

*

Folk have been learning new skills in lockdown.
For the sake of their sanity
I've been banned from the ukulele,
so I've joined Himself for date nights in the shed.
He shows me videos of men going
thunk-thunk-thunk,
tries to teach me *Spin* and *Half-Spin,*

but I prefer my default mode
– fling as hard as I can
in the hope it nails the target.

When he gets three strikes to the heart of his mark,
he looks at me all romantic and says,
ah ... springtime in Paris ...

My Post Lives the Life of My Dreams

I love to track from dispatch,
watch it travel to everywhere we're not allowed to go.

The daughter's iPad cover
sailed across the Irish Sea on the Princess Royal DC.

A sleeveless jacket I bought for Himself-in-the-shed
winged its way over from Hinchley.

Even though his big birthday in Paris was cancelled,
the present of throwing knives flew from Russia

to be stuck in a warehouse in Portadown for a week.
These days – even that's exotic.

STAYING SAFE
for Tom O'Kane and John Lunny

The seventy-something next door
is planted into a sycamore.

His chainsaw roars as he lops
and him stretched out near the top.

With everything at ground-level trim
the other neighbour's up painting the chimney.

His grandson sighs
as he hears him say,

I might walk that roof,
and him well over eighty.

God Bless the Bees

The Mother,
cocooned in Leitrim,
takes out her frustration
on wandering roses
and other wayward strays
who assume
they can travel freely
in the empire of her garden.

She's terrified of bees
or she'd have
the secateurs gripped
in her arthritic hand
while she hoists
her cobalt knee
onto a wobbly stool
to stand and butcher
the bumbled
Berberis darwinii.

JAILBREAK

Feck this cocoon, I'm heading out,
the Mother declares over the phone.

When I ask where she's going
she replies, *the chemist*.

I suggest if she wants
to risk her life

she heads anywhere
but out for tablets.

Bring Olive or Ena to sing along
to their *Choir of Ages* CD.

Go out at full blast
like *Thelma and Louise,*

speeding to the border
in the Yaris.

Corona Calypso

The daughter, in charge of the playlist,
cranked Harry Belafonte up to max.
Harry lifted us off the couch and onto our feet.

As we started to do interpretative dance
the dog joined our conniptions,
barking and biting our arses.

Parrot, a Harry fan,
went buck-mad for calypso,
got onto his outside swing to be swung,

whistled upside down to *Matilda*,
lay on his back in my hand
to be coochie-cooed.

I coochie-cooed,
he coochie-cooed back,
it was all too much for the cat.

The daughter hoked in her box of stuff
to find her rattling egg.
I threw beer bottle caps into a ziplock bag

and we sang as loud as we could.
While she rattled her egg
I shook my cap tambourine to the beat,

Angelina, *Matilda* and *Banana Boat*
on repeat for Parrot,
who whistled along

until he started to nip
and had to be put in
to calm down.

When she's grown up and gone
to a home of her own,
I hope the daughter remembers

what to do when times are tough,
crank it up to max, sing and dance,
no matter what.

The Butcher's Daughter

I'd lost belief, was as low as I'd ever been
when Himself tells me his dream ...

"I dreamt last night you'd organised your annual fight
with the world bare-knuckle boxing champion.

Our road was crowded with bookies, chip vans
and folk having the craic,

the daughter and me, VIPs, our own seats
on account of you going undefeated.

People asked how the yearly bout came to be.
I told them you talked to all sorts as you set up the meet.

They wanted to know where you'd learned
to bare-knuckle fight.

It was just something you did on the border
– a tradition to train the butcher's daughter.

Men eyed me with awe, *a man fit to handle
that kind of woman.*

We were sure this was your year to go down,
for the champ was a bull of a man.

When the fight began
you flattened the bull three times,

and three times the bull rose again
to shouts and cheers

as ye headed over the hill
like Trooper Thorn and Will Danaher.

Those of us used to your fights sat down
for we thought it'd be drawn out like in previous years,

but half an hour later you reappeared,
whistling and swinging your arms

as you marched home over the brow of the hill
alone."

The Stench of Poetry

It's one of those half-light days in November.
We're on the school run in stagnant traffic
when a man walks across Erne Bridge,
has that familiar look – the tortured artist.

I try to place where I've seen him before,
slicked ginger hair, beard, black trousers,
his winter coat,
the blue of *The Starry Night*.

I rouse herself from WhatsApp with a shout,
Look at that man!
He's the spit of Van Gogh!
Imagine, Van Gogh in Enniskillen ...

She pauses mid-message, glances out,
Oh yeah! He is!
I feel words coming on,
start to get carried away,

There's a poem in this! I say,
but Herself doesn't miss a tap,
There'll be no poetry in the car.
We'll never get rid of the smell.

ACKNOWLEDGEMENTS

Thanks to the editors of the following publications in which some of these poems appeared: *Poetry Ireland Review*, *Fortnight Magazine*, *Smithereens*, *The Honest Ulsterman*, *A New Ulster*, *The Leitrim Guardian*, *The Power of Words: Holocaust Memorial e-pamphlet* (Lagan Online), *Poethead* online, Poetry in Motion's *Making Memories*, *Vision*, and *Heartland* anthologies (Community Arts Partnership), *Corncrake Magazine*, *Literati Magazine*, *The Writers' Café*, *The Bangor Literary Journal*, *Borderlines Stickleback* (Hedgehog Poetry Press), *The Bramley* (Flash Fiction Armagh), *North West Words*, *Books Ireland*, *Washing Windows III & IV* (Arlen House), *Epoque Press Ezine*, *Loughshore Lines* (Fermanagh Writers), *The Bee's Breakfast* (Beautiful Dragons Press), *Places of Poetry* (Oneworld Publications), *North Star* (Women Aloud NI), *Gutter Magazine*, *Poems from the Heron Clan VIII* (Katherine James Books), *Local Wonders: Poems of Our Immediate Surrounds* (Dedalus Press), The Impartial Reporter, and *The Polaris Trilogy* (Brick Street Poetry).

A massive thanks to Ruth Carr for encouragement during my first creative writing classes at the Crescent Arts Centre, Belfast in 2008. Thanks to the facilitators of subsequent workshops over the years and to the John Hewitt Society for awarding a bursary to attend the John Hewitt International Summer School in 2016, a transformative experience which set me on the path to taking my writing seriously. I'm indebted to the Fermanagh and Omagh District Council for other JHISS bursaries and funding my first residency at the Tyrone Guthrie Centre. Thanks to Poetry Ireland for a Poetry Town Bursary for a subsequent residency at the TGC. I'm deeply grateful to the directors and all the staff at the TGC. Special mention to Martina Beagan for therapeutic shopping sessions when the going was too tough. Thanks to Paul Maddern at the River Mill and McCall Gilfillan at Space to Write for other writing retreats.

I'm grateful to the Arts Council of Northern Ireland and the National Lottery for funding two SIAP awards and a

Travel Award to perform at the London Irish Centre. Thanks to the Irish Writers Centre for course bursaries, professional membership and a residency at Cill Rialaig, and mentorships with the talented poets Maureen Boyle and Moyra Donaldson. Thanks also to my writer friends and facilitators in the various writing and performance groups I've been involved in for their encouragement, including the Crescent Arts Creative Writers, Fermanagh Writers, Women Aloud NI, Flash Fiction Armagh, The Thing Itself, and The Glen's Centre. Thanks to the Fermanagh Beekeepers for their support. Friends and extended family all over the world have cheered on my real-world and online performances – there are too many to mention, but I'm forever grateful. I owe a debt of gratitude to my neighbours for providing fodder for my writing and the people of Kilty for not disowning me.

Maureen Boyle deserves sainthood for her critique of the manuscript throughout its many revisions and for her excellent guidance and laughs when I needed them most. Thanks to Réaltán Ní Leannáin for her sage advice on Irish translations. My gratitude to Frank Farrelly and Nuala O'Connor for generously reading the manuscript and for amazing blurbs. A special thanks to the trailblazer Marie Jones for telling me to 'get out there, do your thing and quit worrying about what them 'uns think'.

Thanks to my wonderful mother, Frances, who did her best, even if this is how I turned out, and my brother Eugene, who takes after Dad as a master storyteller. I am grateful to him and his brilliant wife, Janny – for being there for family support when I was galivanting at writer retreats and performances.

I wish my mother-in-law, Moira (a harsh critic of subpar writing, yet despite this, my staunchest supporter) was here to critique this book. Thanks to my patient husband, Ronan, whom my father lovingly called 'that poor bastard', and my long-suffering daughter, Sarah, who's mortified at the title even though she inspired it. Finally, thanks to Alan Hayes from Arlen House for taking a chance on *Stench*.

Notes

Stench is divided into three sections, themed around the first verse of Irving Berlin's song, 'Let's Face the Music and Dance' which played when we walked down the aisle at our wedding in Connemara. It embodies our life ethos: laugh in the face of adversity.

p. 21: *10–10–20*, agricultural fertiliser used in the 1970s/1980s.

p. 36: *Galway Crystal:* The church where we were married was built over granite slabs. They couldn't shift the rocks while building the foundations, so the builders left a slope up to the altar.

p. 37: *The Coolin:* An Irish musical air often characterised as one of the most beautiful in the traditional repertoire.

p. 46: *Aunty Nellie's*: Sweet shop in Galway.

p. 48: *The Soul's Veneer:* The poem is meant to be read vertically and horizontally.

p. 50: *Plant*: Another name for a walking stick in Leitrim.

p. 50: *Sheugh*: Ditch or furrow.

p. 66: *African Grey:* A parrot known for their amazing mimicry.

p. 69: *St Angelo Airport:* Enniskillen/St Angelo airport was built during World War II as RAF St Angelo and later renamed St Angelo Barracks while in use as a British Army base. It has been in private ownership as a civilian airport since 1996.

p. 77: *Choir of Ages:* Ireland's renowned concert orchestra conductor and choirmaster, David Brophy, assembled an intergenerational choir from North Leitrim and Crumlin/Walkinstown in Dublin for an RTÉ series in 2017. My mother, Ena Domoney and Olive Gallagher were members of this choir.

p. 81: Trooper Thorn and Will Danaher are characters in the 1952 John Ford movie *The Quiet Man*.

About the Author

Credit: Sheerin Photography

Trish Bennett is a writer and performer who grew up in north Leitrim on the ROI/UK border during The Troubles. Her life, spent in equal parts in Ireland and Northern Ireland, has shaped her into a writer who effortlessly straddles boundaries, being at home on the page or stage. Her writing spans poetry, memoir, and short stories. She delves into a myriad of themes, from the landscape of her people to the comical escapades of her family and other creatures.

She won the Roscommon New Writing Award 2022 and the *Leitrim Guardian* Literary Award for Poetry in 2017 & 2018. Her work has been listed in renowned competitions such as the National Poetry Competition, Mslexia, Fish, Allingham, Trim, and Mono, and was featured on radio/TV and at festivals across Ireland and the UK, including at the London Irish Centre, Cúirt and Culture Night.

Her poetry is widely published in the UK, Ireland and the USA. Her winning poem, 'Staying Safe', was published in postcard format by Dedalus Press. 'Sweet Spot' featured in the BBC & Ulster Orchestra's 40th anniversary show at the Ulster Hall. 'The Stench of Poetry' is part of a Lunar Codex of poetry and art headed to the moon on a 2025 NASA flight.

In 2019, Hedgehog Poetry Press published *Borderlines*, a micro-pamphlet. *Stench* is her debut collection.